What's in a Name?

Poems by

Nich

Front and division illustrations by Ricky Powell, Jr.

1st run, February 2019, Hampton Roads, Virginia
Copyright © 2019 Nicholis Williams
1st edition   ISBN: 9798618130066
2nd edition ISBN: 978-1-952773-19-8

"Born in the world low as a cloud from secondhand
cocaine powder,
the clairvoyant infant is stripped from God
and labeled a statistic.
Endowed by joy and seeing what lies
beneath, coherently smiled in the face of radical
dividends, while being preyed upon by the panic
button
of monsters too scared to sleep with their own
shadow.
Four winters
on the electric strip had come and gone until his soles
bled blue.
Cemented blocks labeled him an insurgent
prior to the disastrous wedding of the season.
Shockingly,
the price on happiness skyrocketed to the
upper east side.
And refugee was shot at those forgotten
memoirs of society.
Barracuda left a bottomless dent on the
battlefield and the knights had taken his piece.
No
longer plugged in, the world turned upside down, and
he cut the TV off."

To whomever is reading this, be warned, for the story you're about to read is the first-hand account of raw humanity in a very complex, yet nonchalant and poetic standpoint. The views addressed in the aforementioned passages reflect the thoughts of an individual's aging, and his under-standing of what exists and what is definite reality. Some of the material may not rub the reader in the comfortable manner, however every thought is recorded with an unbiased mind in account, irregardless of the topics at hand. This work of art is a culmination of various persons, ideas, scenarios, consequences, lessons, achievement, failures and growth.
Hope you enjoy the journey,
Nich.

contents

Nich

Nich

Now do you Understand?

I don't speak fast you're just listening slow
Possums have rabies, along with raccoons
Spades are my second tongue so don't challenge me
And football is in my blood, I just have high metabolism

I don't swim with gators
I've yet to build a shack
However, I do love gumbo, and my feet are flat
I say y'all with everything so refrain from correcting me

Grits can be eaten for dinner and breakfast
There's a drawl in my words, and yes I'm aware
Unless you record me I CAN'T HEAR MY ACCENT I swear
Slow paced doesn't mean I grew up on a farm
I'm modestly polite, guess it's my southern charm
I don't eat pig fat and I don't sleep with my cousins
How many times I have to repeat myself…

I'M NOT COUNTRY I'M SOUTHERN!

[1] Visited Ohio, Jun. '15

I HATE New York

The novel of eight million chapters full
of non stop construction interrupting my sleep
The crowded sidewalks and congested transportation methods
Not to mention, the over-priced muffins
And sewer rats; seriously what are they eating!
The endless tourist with pointless questions
And trigger happy fuck-ups who're scared to lose a fight
Five boroughs of mischief and two-faced coins
It sucks waking up in the city that never sleeps.

Chasing Pavements

I love to watch you dance. It's as if the wind plays the electric
slide and you're the first on the dance floor. You scream
freedom across the sky; so carefree and wild. Though idle from
time to time, you're always appreciated

As your glum eyes weep, I sit with you, awaiting the beauty
beyond those melancholic cries. There are days I won't see you
cause I know you're out being a hero, so I sit and wait.

I love to watch you draw. By far, nothing has come close to your
masterful techniques. Such elegance leaves me in awe. A fata
morgana of the illustrious Shangri - La
miles above the cemented floor. Just you and I until the ends of
the earth.

I love the sound of your voice. When you sing, it's as if 1000 butterflies are harmonizing Aretha Franklin down to the finest octave. Powerful enough to stretch the globe if you listen close enough.

I am truly your greatest subjugate. One day I'll glide my hands across your curves and carve my name onto your luxurious figure. Wiping the dew from my face, raising myself up to your zenith, easing through your highway swimmingly.

As for me, well, I still have a few stones left to overturn.

<u>Home</u>

They say home is where the heart is and perhaps that's true.
Can I make a quick call so I can phone home too?
If it's not too much of a burden may I sleep on your couch.
See my heart ran away when I was put out the house,
By a woman who never loved me, yet claimed that she did
I was nothing in her eyes and I was only a kid.
I won't stay long I promise it just isn't my style
I guess I never really have a reason for actually sticking around.

"Perhaps I was addicted to the dark side,
somewhere inside my childhood I missed my heart die."

Orchid

I hear when you love someone that you
should drop a rose on their behalf.
But when the soil used for fertilization
is corrupted by the empty, lifeless souls,
that once were foundations of a beautiful
garden, you begin to wonder.
Just how did a rose grow from concrete?

Leftovers

You were a soggy bowl of lucky charms
when secretly I preferred French Toast.

You walked around like gold plated filet
mignon without realizing you were a
Peking duck, foul, and made me nauseous.

I remember you compared us to Shrek,
but after the fifth layer, I should've hit
myself with an iron skillet for thinking
onions won't make you cry.

Even the best of chefs stumble in the
kitchen. Although, I highly doubt they
continue after a grease fire burns the
last supper and all that's left are the
ramen noodles in the cabinet.

I would fantasize about the times we
made coffee. Light on the sugar, a dash
of honey, with lots of cream, oh and
don't forget the cinnamon. However, you
became thirsty, and would sneak off and
sip tea with a former flame.

Honestly, it was kinda fun playing the
oblivious fool, but it's not called sage for
show. You say you dreamt of apple pies in
fresh spring meadows, and spoke highly
of mountains covered in butter pecan ice
cream. Too bad a sugar rush causes
slight hallucinations.

I tried to shower you in lavender
lemonade with fresh mint leaves on top,
but you wouldn't drink. I offered you warm
brownies, yet you claimed fudge made
your throat itchy. When I was down to my
last slice, you snatched it up and threw
it away for being cold. So please, once I
raise my fork don't look my way.

You had a chance to indulge in this
banquet, but you were too naive and
greedy. I hope the cookie jar was worth
it.

[5] Saw Big K.r.i.t. in concert, Jul. '15

Intermission

Where was my cheerful smile?
What happened to my sense of
assurance?
It's as if God was using my bones to
orchestrate the saddest song I've ever felt.
Endless days spent wasting valuable breath spitting half
eaten truths and swallowing lies I tell myself.
Eventually, I broke down, and cried myself to sleep.
I awoke to a new light, a man on a mission, a boy no more.
This was the setback I needed!

~~Scars~~

Truthfully, I couldn't conjure up the.
strength to seek out your forgiveness.
Because deep down I knew I didn't
deserve it .

[6] First comedy show, Oct. '15

...

I want to fuck the shit out of her insecurities until
the beauty of her soul spills onto the covers that
she hides under… until she lays there… stripped
of her flaws lying ass naked in her desirability.

Then perhaps, I would attempt… to take her clothes off.

I ask her, when was the last time someone ran their fingers through the knots of your soul?

She speak novels to me topless while I rest between her legs, rubbing her vagina, watching her words turn into moans that scream intelligence.

"Ethereal"

I live in this invisible world, unknown to those I come into contact with.

A place with never ending sunsets, simply because I want to bask in the beauty of the dancing star;

A void of timeless symphonies and memories that dance along the deserted shadows.

I walk in silence; forgetful how the world sounds for a brief moment. A laconic voice, sturdy, but very lackadaisical naps on my shoulder,

What's in a Name?

Nich

I haven't quite got the concept of
raising my words... or voice for that
matter.

If only I could step out of this realm into
that of humanity? But why rally
alongside skeletons full of burden?

Why breathe in a world of toxicity that'll
plague my sacred temple?

Incarcerate my thoughts and rupture my
being, it all sounds so uncanny!

The ability to perceive what others call
illusions, and feel mom's heartbeat.

I've always wondered, if animals could
talk, what would I say to them,

Or, if life came with its own set of
instructions for me would I follow it?

Perhaps time will answer this with the
plethora of hour glasses now
shattered before me.

Broken foundations creep over vast
clouds that rattle the very fabric of
this reality...

Perhaps the sky might fall... one day.
I always knew I could fly, hypothetically
of course!

Until I realized wings are manifestations
created to diminish dreams of
escape,

And bumps in the night were one
bogeyman away from schizophrenia.

For a decade, I've wanted to be invisible,
not transparent but surrounded.

By the guardians of before, now
belittled by the evils of transformation.

The astral plane below my soles reflect
the motions above my crown.

A hollow heartbeat echoes throughout
my body, causing my nerves to tingle.

I should step out of this cast and let the
butterfly free

Unfortunately, my atrabilious attitude
prevents such phenomenon.

So I sit here and watch the trees cry, as
battle scars prance atop their canopy.

Souls battered and burned for
thousand of years, yet unwavering eyes
dismiss the actions of tyrant ancestry.

If life came with a restart button I'd
hesitate to touch it, only because I know
what lies beyond the shutter.

Nich

Silent screams of blasphemy ring
throughout the atmosphere.

Can you hear them? Ignore the smog
and calm your mind.

I died while reaching out for you, not
knowing trenches can easily fill with
quicksand.

A lost traveler guided by the stars,
crashing into cliffs, and swallowed by
aquatic beasts,

Because the lighthouse flashes at the
wrong second,
and the moon refuses to shine a glimmer
of hope, so I drift…

Away from my last chances at
redemption, retribution, and revival.

Nevertheless, I smile.

I yearn for the days where 525,948.766
rotations won't be spent dreaming of
what ifs.

But the movement of my psyche
labels me a being.

Where my voice carries bombs of
encouragement over treacherous terrain,
and my words go to war with Apollo
Creed himself.

Watch as people compliment each other
without a hint of envy,

And pride is nothing more than a gang of
majestic lions on the prowl to maintain
dominance in the food chain.

When someone tells you they love you,
and actually mean it,

and being concerned shows I'm hueman.

Laughter will cure cancer and bullets
will disassemble before they strike flesh...

and my elder self will appear as a reflection of
foreshadowing.

We'll converse about the times when
everything made sense... over a bowl of gumbo.

And I'll inscribe every word in my brain,
tattooed on grey matter and axons,

looking back at the road I traversed
only stopping to tie my shoe.

Behold, a jewel as precious as air, engulfing
the void of emptiness left to wither in time.

As kaleidoscope personas of alertness
and aloofness dance along my shadow...

I guess, all good things do come in threes.

[9] Found out Marvin's a genius, Oct. '15

[10] Started spoken word book, Nov. '15

"Moonlight"

Today is tomorrow's yesterday that I've
been waiting for, and in the process of
letting go, I realized what was and what
was never there to begin with.

I ponder aimlessly, if I'm not in control,
then who is? I sleep on words
that go let unspoken, unbeknownst
the reason for my insomnia.

Why do we always end up thinking about
our lives at night? It's as if that's when
everything stops, and the only noise you
hear is a slow heartbeat.

Moved by gust of future endeavors,
yet struck of mnemonic faults.
I fear one day that when I look
back, I'll only see my breath and pulse,
instead of a life truly lived.

Life shoots bullets that I can't dodge,
and reality, well it's a book I never bother
to finish reading.

"Rose"

Love;
a small word with a loud voice,
producing more bass than the largest
amphitheater, and built
like the wind.
It can knock you off your feet or cool
your warm sensations.
Its, watching cartoons in bare freedom
eating quesadillas beside your
best friend,
balancing the weight of clouds at the
speed of air currents...
a true rush of overflowing passion!
But don't forget to buckle up.
You'll travel noctambulous speeds through
endless tunnels and open highways,
so fill the tank up, the ride's the best
part.
It's one more page; an open book
of timeless chapters floating over
bended pages along the ruffled creases
of an obstructing canvas.
It's absolutely comical!
Pointless jokes that give rise to one's
libido.
Mellifluous gestures that spark insanity, and patience
is a blue ocean floor of cascading thoughts.
So set sail for tomorrowland, we embark
at dawn.
It's infinitive art.

Nich

The melodies a heartbeat sing while sculpting
masterpieces,
an anesthetic of trusting hands towards
crippled hearts.
Cerebral ascension on a everlasting scale,
just two beams of consciousness traveling
at frequencies of light.
An equilibrium of ecstasy over the
geometric grid, I suppose.
Love is...when I gaze into your eye
and feel like a kid again.
So please, pardon me when I stare,
things of such beauty tend to leave me
breathless.
Funny,
I spoke of God as nothing more than a
fairy tale, that is, until the day I met
you.

[11] Visited North Carolina, Dec. '15

...

She teased my ego as she twirled her
tongue around my earlobe, bragging of
the magic that lay dormant between her
thighs. Tsk, if only she knew the things I
could do with my tongue.

Our eyes connect. Galaxies scream from
her pupils as I lean forward, pressing my
lips onto her velvet like flesh. Truthfully,
her moan was the first time I heard real
music.

[12] Got a tattoo, Feb. '16

˜IKIGAI˜

It can be difficult to get out of bed
when you can't find a reason to. There
will be some days where you won't feel
capable of getting up. So just lay there
and breathe. As long as you're breathing,
it's okay. But you can never stop breathing.
No matter how bad it gets or how lost
you feel. You have to breathe. If it's the only
thing you do some days, that's fine.
Because you're still here. Breathing doesn't
always mean you'll feel alive, but you'll
still be here, and that's the most important
thing of all.

"BUD(d)(y)"

A (p)(o)(u)(n)(d) of misunderstanding rest heavy on my chest
S(o)(u)(r) thoughts ooze through my hair follicles leaving a
woozy haze across my membrane
B(u)(d)(d)(h)(a) becomes my shadow as I breathe a new leaf

...a bright spark makes way to a new flame...

The aura of your aroma fills my
nostrils creating (p)(s)(y)(c)(h)(e)(d)(e)(l)(i)(c) pleasures
I taste you in my thoughts and
breathe out ecstasy

What's in a Name?

Nich

Your (e)(x)(o)(t)(i)(c) tongue sucks the saliva
from my mouth making me want you more
So let's (r)(o)(l)(l) (u)(p) and cuddle the night away,
A (g)(o)(d)(d)(e)(s)(s), all natural in shape
Pure euphoria!

Twenty is a helluva drug...

Nich

Jovial Decisions

If irenic motives drove you to
the avenues of hypothetical
reunification, where love sleeps
on the sidewalk, and telesthetic
nightmares walk freely down the
boulevard, with tre pounds ready
to empty four chambers that'll leave
a trail of crimson paint on the baron
asphalt then consider this…

Would you pull the trigger?

[15] Jumped at trampoline park, May '16

|NICKTIONARY|

apostasy: a total desertion of or departure from
one's religion, principles, party, cause, etc.

ANNO LUCIS

Everyday I wake up, wipe the history from
my face, and brush the legalese of yesternight
from my breath.

Moonwalking out to the solar ambiance
that hugs my spiritual presence, I jaunt
my way through this metaphysical realm,
carefully planning my next move.

What's in a Name?

See a perfectionist is the greatest procrastinator,
which makes time the ultimate factor of mental
obedience,

therefore, I choose to art my way between the
lines.

Walking in such godly stature, I feel my skin
reflect the cosmic consciousness I absorb
from the everlasting noble.
I'm able hold my own with sadistic forces trying
to mine the treasures I have amassed over
celestial revolutions.

I am moor than a name, and no number will
determine the length of my existence.

My volition has been written ever so clearly.
The brave warrior sheathed long ago is now ready
to roar his voice across
the skies.

This is my year of golden exploration, consider
this my affidavit.

[19] Went to Cedar Point, Jun. '16
[20] Explored the sand dunes in North Carolina, Jun.'16

-Testimony-

If I could, I would talk to you for hours on end about the stars in the sky, whether aliens exist, or why we're unable to vibrate at such frequencies as to where, animal sounds are no longer foreign to the nimiety of dialects we speak.

I'd speak of dogmatic principles staked into the hearts of gentle minds, and how we swim the darkness, oblivious to the only explanation we know of light is because our planet turns to its closest star. Alas, I finally innerstood why the caged bird sings.

But, I'd rather converse freely in my thoughts, writing poetry, of all the things I have trouble saying. At least that way, I know you'll always respond to my foolishness.

Revolutionary Act

If being misunderstood was a common practice then Tookie would be the posterboy, and I guarantee Huey would lead the campaign…

Imagine if you will, uninterrupted life transition when a familiar sensation triggers past memories of a story never lived. You then rewind through words inscribed onto the fabrics of reality as if you've read them personally from pieces of decayed wooden flesh. However, you just became an adult and this is doubled your life years. Freaky right?

What's in a Name?

With all this truth in my life I swear people think I gangbang, slide cause my flag hang, and peace god with my left hand. It's just the light to freedom antagonizes casualties of war and truthfully, I'm just too high to riot. Because common sense has become so illogical that it almost seems chosen if you ask me. Now make no mistake about it, revolution is a dangerous process, but the destruction of oppression sure is an incipient sight in this crab barrel society.

Suicidal thoughts bombard illusionary ideologies of recurring progression, as I sit and reminisce the days when fruits were pure and the skies were true. Oblivious to the fact I grew up on a stomach filled with bleach washed lunch trays stocked full of foreign falsification, while simultaneously, drinking eight glasses of fluoride until my eyes calcify beyond comprehension. Pathological recipes enriched in aspartame and atrazine created noteworthy pies made to cripple my subconscious ego. An undercover attempt to quarantine a being so that I no longer bred fruit from the tree of life, because the darker the berry, the sweeter the juice, and melanin by far tastes the sweetest.

As I snapped out the matrix, I fully understood the game of cognitive chess being played from sunup to sundown. In order to trap the king you first have to play the game. Be strategic, too many openings allows one to force your hand. When all's said and done, only the strong shall remain. Reclaim the kingdom with grace and branch onto new lands.

I'm spraying knowledge with my finger on the trigger, hollow tips fly from banana clips since I refuse to be another nigger. Martyrdom became the product of peaceful equations in this divisional state, where educational institutions prescribe obedience duendes to eradicate royal consciousness.

Taxed freedom with no signature molded brains from the ripe, as nescience media programming played puppeteer to a generation in the making. And numeric encoding sold televised puppets with words plagued full of action verbs to define the modern-day change.

Funny, only change I know consists of these metallic zombies I carry in my wallet in case I get thirsty. Truth be told, I've yet to buy anything with real currency. Everything I have was bought with pieces of time I sold from my life to a corporation that will never have paid me enough once my time is up. Capitol currency planted paper planes around the globe dropping nickels and dimes of IOUs, ironically, no one noticed the monopolist presidential color scheme turning you against your neighbor.

Secret agendas hidden in plain sight fuel silent killers raged by infamy, to wage war on the oppressed minds of those claiming it "protects." Its called law enforcement until there's two shooters. A gun without a badge is a murder weapon. Bullets that lay in blue shirts are confirmed kills. Brown bodies in the ground, casualties of war. Tears only wash the concrete, the blood dyes pants and t- shirts. My mind is certain they'll take all they can get, so push their buttons and hit reset. Cultural appropriation, muffled cries on deaf ears, and stolen lands are just the tip of the iceberg. That bootstrap theory doesn't fit on all those feet. Much like glutton. Starving pigs. No lives matter, save the babies, before
NO LIVES MATTER!

Now do I have your attention, or are you merely confused? Rebuke! For everything I quote rest labyrinths of truth. Watch and behold as the story unfolds. From diamond and pearls to cities of gold. Different eyes see different lies, yet go uncovered for. Smothered by the false flags of daily smorgasbord of information that does not contain clarification over what came first: The chicken or the egg?

What's in a Name?

Why burn bridges if you can't swim the rivers beneath? If I say Cesare wasn't god would I die in my sleep? Because the matrix so deep we think it's 2016, but then again, you can't see oxygen, but believe you can breathe.

So take heed when I stand tall and say; FUCK all the thugs who play judge, jury, and executioner.
FUCK the thugs that claim executive, legislative, and judicial.
FUCK all the misguided idols.
FUCK those twice that destroy families with loaded rifles.
And FUCK those in denial. FREE those encaged by bibles so they may scrape the crown of paganism and prosper.

With government sucking the dicks of corporations, it looks like Uncle Sam finally put his money where his mouth is.

Now, before I take this smoke break,
I'm asseverate my words won't go unspoken.
Henceforth,
don't paint me BLACK when I used to be GOLDEN.

[23] First apartment, Nov. '16

<random post #21>
Ever wonder if the people you're observing realize they're standing next to a splitting image of themselves? Whether it be different ages or complexion, it's like looking through an invisible mirror.

~PSALMS OF AN UNDERACHIEVER~

I just wanna meditate to coolie high, crumblin erb, screaming the world is mine, with thugs mansion echoing through the whispers of the wind. I'll never forget the way I looked into the mirror and said no more tears. I ban them from ever leaping from my eye sockets. On my own accord, I testify, the God smile is all I'm searching for. The knowing of what's to come in this present-day. Yea, that's the key.

~ Flatbush Ave ~

Under the shade of the Brooklyn tree,
I found solace with the mango seed.
I watch it grow, and sprout it roots, not
realizing it was I you see. I set my time
of 365 and after that I vacate. I'll leave a
man, with lessons learned, a year filled
with so much outbreak. Its freshman year,
the sun is warm, and girls are ready to breed.
I sip fine wine in Brooklyn times and toast to
mango seed!

What's in a Name?

|NICKTIONARY|
strawman: a fictional legal entity, created with the hope that as a child grows up, he/she will be fooled into believing that he/she is actually the strawman (in which he/she most definitely is not) and pay all sorts of imaginary costs and liabilities which get attached to the strawman.

DISTANT Relatives

Is it because 7,917.5 miles make us distant relatives, or because CHNOPS are the cardinal points in the sustainability of our development? Either or, I'm glad to say:

"I pledge allegiance to the earth of our beloved solar system.
And to all of her creatures, for here they dwell, one planet,
united in harmony, with
universal love."

Dear Earthling,
I anticipate the day we converse once more. Although our words adjoined briefly a second, the essence of your truths still resonate in the atmospheric pressure which flows out of my lungs, as I exhale the brutality, and breathe a new oasis.

Dear Earthling,
Your flesh no longer satisfies the mental hold of global dominance which has caused much turmoil throughout the eras. I no longer wish to take part in the eradication of your conscious being. Henceforth, the removal of repetitive headaches eating away at my psyche.

Dear Earthling,
The world isn't fairy tales and castles. I just wish you saw the bigger picture.

Dear Earthling,
Two years of mutual aging brought forth much respected growth. Your appearances may have changed, but ultimately, you remained the same. Maybe time does heal all wounds. Thank you for not giving up on me.

Dear Earthling,
I see you played your madness card so I'll raise you some compassion and understanding. Pharmaceutical compressors prescribed with water did cripple and make you hard to manage. I heard your pain. I felt your troubles. More than ever, I'll never turn my back one way or another.

Dear Earthling,
My masked emotions for you are coming forward and I'm afraid you'll judge them prematurely before the finished project.

Dear Earthling,
You created a monster and now you shame the consequences. Tender loving and care were the most essential methods needed for progression. There was no need for any shortcuts.

Dear Earthling,
I wish I was able to vibrate at such frequencies, as to where, your native tongue is no longer foreign to the nimiety of dialects we speak.

Dear Earthling,
One season every quinquennium, your incipient roots break free of the corroded soil bringing a new breath to an empty chest plain, carefully carving the landscapes above. I wish others would understand the tedious processes you'll inherit

Nich

throughout your lifespan. Maybe then would they finally innerstand your tears.

Dear Earthling,
Your beauty is out of this world spectacular. You are the epitome of stunning. A queen in a her godly rite. The sunset that rests over the ocean. A rose dipped in chocolate and coated with diamonds.

Dear Earthling,
You have been the most random, energetic. bundle of pure excitement I've happen to come across. I hope you understand that I cherished your vibe greatly.

Dear Earthling,
You will ALWAYS be my best friend no matter how old we get.

Dear Earthling,
You heart is filled with so much compassion and truth that I wonder where do you have place for oxygen. You'll eagerly give your last to someone in need, and take in any lost soul finding its path.

~Sturgeon Moon~

And when it was time to bid our farewells,
you grabbed my hand and begged for me
to stay. I reach forward wiping the tears from your
face and say goodbyes are a thing of the past.
Next time we meet, I'll be a better man.

[Appreciation Letter]

To whomever you may be,

I want you to know I love you and that everything will be ok,
I want you to know I love you and I'm glad that you're here
today.

I want you to know I love you so all your pain can disappear,
I want you to know I love you for still being here.
I want you to know I love you although we've never truly met,
I want you to know I love you so you can continue without
regrets.

I want you to know I love you through the seasons
and the pain,
I want you to know I love you even if I don't know your name.

I want you to know I love you because love is for all,
I want you to know I love you even in your worst downfall.

I want you to know I love you because love has no end,
I want you to know I love you so now we can be friends.

I want you to know I love you as vast as the sky is big,
I want you to know I love you like a playground loves kids.

I want you to know I love you and this we won't debate,
Because love is universal and I love to appreciate.

No matter what happened, is happening, or will happen, I know
one thing that's for sure.
We're all in this together, so long as the love is pure.

[24] Visited Georgia, Jan. '17

atom & Eve

Fused with dark matter and vested with cosmic rays.
Tuned by galactic power and adorned with grace.
Stronger than a thousand suns and venerated by it's
praise.
Omniscient with knowledge of self, and immutable to
change.
A voice of many waters, thunder and lightning befitting
names,
watch the crown as he walks and proudly
HE WILL REIGN.
A god amongst men is what's being explained. A god
amidst men only shines from god's veins.

Adam chose Eve is what I've
been told to believe when in
reality, atom expands through
the wave of quintessence. Eve
has been, and always will be, but
Adam tricks the heart into false
imprisonment.
Cause love is (her)e.

To overstand a woman's purpose is to first know
her origin. She is older than any known languages,
and is the demiurge of all terrestrial planets. She's the
elder scroll that inspires all men to write. She's the
scriptures of our life.
Mother of god, and creator of the all.

She is the El Kuluwm from womb to tomb.
Now ask yourself, aren't all constellations, stars, and
their life forms birthed?
RESPECT HER CROWN!
For she's the triple dark mother mother

~Outliers~

I fancy the weird individuals.
Those deemed black sheep.
The complete oddballs.
Those of whom breathe in the left field.
The moonflowers, the underdog, the
solitary players.
Those of whom society rejected as outcast.
The outsiders who don't care to peak
through the looking glass.
The ugly ducklings, the eccentric valves.
The shattered pieces of stained glass
laid out in a beautiful mosaic.
The invisible anomalies.
Someone proud to be a walking, talking,
conundrum.
And those who feel lost and forgotten
about.

That's why one day I'll let my jolly roger
grace the sky, and break bread with those
who starved before me.

[25] I'm no longer a baby cousin, Nomtoc '17

~*Limbo*~

Coming of age in a world that doesn't
want me to blossom sure does take a toll on my senses.
Statistics say I achieved greatness while
reality hit me with a brutal six am wake up call.
A life almost wasted over an accident never
thought to happen threw me back 10 paces on the chessboard,
and I found myself spinning in circles,
going nowhere fast. In order for me to reach a state of peace
from this cryptic mindset, I had to transition
myself into a new environment, and grow at my own pace.

Free of anger and exoskeletal disbelief, I
expelled myself from the underbelly of the beast, and began my
search for a more in-tune innerstanding
of my surroundings. But where should I begin?

I vowed I'll go from a boy on a mission
to a man with a purpose, who fights litigation and camouflage
knights, trying so desperately to silence
my image. Minutes turned into days which in turn became
weeks that cruised into months of stagnant
progression. It feels as if I'm slowly crying myself into a river of
sorrow, along with the rest of empty souls
crashing together in the ocean. I trip over countless bumps
etched into the cement on my way down the yellow
brick road, and take detours too dangerous for oneself to
explore
alone.

This empty place is only a figment of my
imagination is what I tell myself… just don't feed the fears.
My eyes are stained crimson from the
pain they endure as I walk this lonely road with no destination
in sight. Time no longer exist. Im staring
into this empty shot glass while the devil's nectar and heaven's
bloom battle throughout my bloodstream.
Scenes of yesteryear replay constantly across my vision and
one thought runs laps around my anatomy...

How, and where can I exit the rabbit hole?

|NICKTIONARY|

false flag: a government sponsored, staged event blamed
on a political enemy and used as a pretext to start a war and/or
enact draconian laws in the name of national security
psychological warfare against citizens of the same
government.

Narcoleptic

Clouded thoughts brewed from the mother's palm, opened my
eye to the nebulous lightscreen being sprayed over the masses
with inconspicuous intentions.
For too long, clandestine operations have taken place in covert
dialects to keep a generation numb. Rewritten lies influence a
gap of malleable minds into the walking dead, and sometimes it
makes me wonder what's really apocalyptic.

Nich

Is it the crash of the dollar, or the zombie epidemic?

"Chosen ones" are breaking the code of conduct to deliver the message for tomorrow, but ears have turned blind to the sounds of reality. Instead of brains filled to the apex with progressive knowledge, we fester in the depths of mass media manipulation, sipping in pools of plagiarized confessions.

Is the sky inexplicably the limit, or have we been bamboozled to a point of disbelief?

Pledged democracies no longer roll off the tongues of we awakened receivers. Those malevolent words fell short with the casualties of dead bodies buried under kinfolk. Terrorism, deceit, and subjugation paint the flag I once respected, now all that's left is a cold shoulder.
Cold summers drag the warm winters down the continual fall slopes, as spring births the same habituation. Causing the three prime spires to react globally to subdue civilization, because bank receipts printed in blood demoralize characteristics of the human population.

So theoretically I wonder, are the images we protrude into the clouds above simply reflective dimensions of the world's below the sea?

Quarries and gravel mines paint the landscape of a beautiful world laid to rest twice upon a time. The planet engraved into our meek minds is nothing more than a treasure trove of mineral deposits that the evils that be claim are untouchable. And so called oceans are imaginative pools of bottomless depth that covered the past in a liquid mummified state.

Therefore I ask, if the dream is sold on a two-sided coin, when it lands, will the outcome be any different?

At 84 minutes past the 19th hour, the alarm clocks began to sing, and it was time to wake up. Were you one of those who pressed the snooze button?

Encephalon: a new wave

It amazes me how sixty pauses
of perception can define my existence.
Other than the fact it takes roughly,
three hundred thirty six hours
prior, for molecular multiplication
to mirror itself millions of times
over. As if infinity was mathematically
probable on a miniscule scale. And
they say one is a lonely number.

Meditate on that for a second...

[32] Climbed a mountain, Jun. '17

What's in a Name?

Nich

~ if god should talk ~

Wake up if you can hear me
Please wake up if you can
The time is surely approaching
For us to reconquer our land

The skies have been distorted
The seas are vastly polluted
The grains are chalked full of poison
And it's all apart of the blueprint

They're killing us for a sport
The media claims it entertainment
Our planet is slowly dying off
Just like the far distant planet

The sun seems holographic and
I'm already missing its joy
The "weather" is often too bipolar
from the courtesy of HAARP

False profits get us rowdy and false
prophets are to blame
While bitch made badge holders are
putting baby supernovae to slain

Shame!
Birth certificates aren't affidavits
neither are licenses you see
Because I self law am master to the
whole 33rd degree

Preach what you teach and quote
what you happen to sow
Since "his"tory is a fallacy and I fight
for it to be told

The paradigm of a 3/5ths is merely
incomplete to the senses
For ancestors knew answers yet kept
all the information hidden

Remember when Pompeii burned up in
ashes and Atlantis feel to the depths
Then the maui on Easter island buried
themselves and constantly wept

It was the early 1300s when
Caucasians came over yonder
They bought germs and bibles as
the men began to wander

They saw temples, gold plated,
and out the woodwork
Envy crept in so they forced us to
go and do work

Broke backs, changed names, and
kept us all masqueraded
Then plantations popped up and life
became a hellish slavery

We'll fist fight kin like to weed out
all the posers, MLK turned the other
cheek and they gave him the cold
shoulder

What's in a Name?

Huey fought back cause they treated
him like an animal,
Killed off his black cubs and left the
black panther to the cannibals

Malcolm had a plan and my brother said fuck
integration them devils only care about a
melanated free nation

~wednesday~

The double digit time paradigm of reality
just hit me square in the face.
I bob and weave and protect myself,
but still catch haymaker hooks with my eyes wide open.

A title fight for proper intelligence hangs in the balance.
Life is the referee counting me out as I arise and continue my
battle nonetheless.

Sweet dear Isis, I thought today was the orchestra of a celestial
day.
An hiatus in the chaos of another 168 hours.
The day a new star was born in the galaxy.

Ironically, as bad as it may sound, I've grown accustomed
to the blows. I call it...wednesday.

This is my Twenty One gun salute.

Nich

WAVELENGTHS & PHOTOGRAPHS

You know you'll be able to tip your hat when you've found friends whose characteristics your personality would go to war for. The ones that'll help you rewrite the constitutional reference of what O'hana means. Where home is a vibrational pattern of echoes and vowels no matter how far you travel. And distance is only millimeters when it comes to being their shadow so that the world doesn't knock them down.

/Verse 1:\

I hope the sentiments in the passage don't come across the wrong way, but this is the passion behind the strength of a friendship that paints new portraits onto empty canvases.

The <u>southern</u> key wields the most raw power they say, and is home to an A-list strategist, willing to ride for the cause. There's no doubt about your character in the eyes of someone who sees the soul you truly are.

/Verse II:\

If I were to have a twin and we separated at birth, lived in close proximity our entire lives, and reunited 18 years later in the chance of an opportunity, would you believe me?

Siamese parallels can perfectly describe the paths we happened to walk once we understood the proper way to put your left foot first. <u>Skywalking</u> sure become an enjoyable treatment afterwards.

What's in a Name?

/Verse III:\

It was four years ago when our paths crossed one another on the island away from our crowded communities. Two years later, our reunion brought forth a bond never thought possible..

You learned me to a world I never thought I would find so intriguing. Your charisma is definitely on super saiyan level, hovering just slightly under the earth's magnetic strip. Northern lights outline the pettiness paved with good intentions.

/Quad Verse:\

I would never turn my back or turn you down even if you turn around. Mí hermaño, friends are created but family is made. And blood couldn't make us any more related.

The originator of the word friend begins with you. The struggle of maintaining communication was my biggest challenge. It took a college acceptance letter for me to truly understand the friend I made. You filled the Zero space that was left when everyone threw me aside. And for that, I thank you.

/Verse V:\

My love for you is beyond measure and I'll overcome any obstacle to ensure your well-being. My friend, your mere presence is enough to turn a gloomy day on its side, and bring forth new adventures. My big homie, I salute you.

/Sixth Verse:\

Our views are swaying us in different directions albeit we're looking through the same window. Home will always be where the heart is, no matter how far we seem to travel.

/Verse VII:\

Our first encounter rubbed me the wrong way and I tried my best to avoid you. Over time however, I've grew fond of your trustworthiness and acknowledge you as my brother.

/Eighth Verse:\

Leaves from divine falling so slow. Like fragile bullet shells drifting in the cold. Brave little soldier boy went marching on. Brave little soldier boy came marching home.

/Verse IX:\

Telekinesis touches keep you in my heart and I still crave your presence even to this day. The only one who can lift up elephants with a simple whisper in the wind, and move clouds with the twinkle of an eye. You're the sister I never want to lose, and the person whose friendship I hold so dearly.

/Verse 10:\

A year has gone and my trust has grown out to a root I call my little. A floriferous chrysanthemum angel graced her presence upon my path and introduced me to a whole new spectrum. New chapters skywrite in my daydreams of the new horizons to be continued.

[33] Visited California, Jul. '17

[34] Experienced a solar eclipse, Aug. '17

CONCRETE NOMAD

Everywhere I seem to roam
I'll come across a Bedouin
being.
The realistic, present day
airbender.
Pushing air and moving hastily
from quadrant to quadrant,
hoping to see another
sunrise.
Simply asking for help in these
desolate times.

I witness the constant transfer
of worthless pieces of paper
leave their hand, because the
stench of their adventures
won't allow them to even put
a foot in the door.
That is, if they have one of
course.

Invisible to the populous that
only an acute amount can see.
What story comes with the
plethora of blankets they
keep?
Have you crossed the path roads
of longevity perhaps?
Questions arise on the bus ride
moving forward.
So long to another no name
nomad.

ATMOSPHERIC MEMOIRS

I am in love with the sky I love how every
night we are painted a new picture
Constant artwork, and all I have to do is
look up
I like how it takes the light so long to reach
me that I am staring at the past
There was so much time between when you
and I were born and when we met
The question is how do you explain your life
to someone?
And the answer is with much difficulty
I am the dark space between the stars
Nothing at first, but zoom in and there
are galaxies upon galaxies hidden inside
Every story I tell you is not so I can be laid
out in a timeline
They are so you can know who I am and
why I have become this way
The memories I share with you are veiled
with connotations that I desperately want
you to understand
I am not a list of events
I am a feeling
I like the sky cause it is meant to be felt
I like the sky because as cliché as it is,
We are sharing it
Looking up at the same story
Told over and over again
In a million different ways.

[35] Tripped on 'shrooms, Aug. '17

What's in a Name?

Nich

brown medusa

You are worth more than a hand-written cordate letter.
More harmonious than a random trip to the beach at
eventide. A painting that says more than a thousand
words.
The essence of a kaleidoscopic breath.

Whether it be the melanin screaming off your skin.
The plumpness of your seducing lips.
The amber dipped constellations taking shelter
in your eyes.
The curve of your voluptuous hips.
The sunshine in your infinite smile.
The power of your gentle mind.
The trust in your understanding hands.
Or,
the passion that flows throughout your heart
so effortlessly.
Is what truly defines a goddess.

[39] Visited Florida, Nov. '17

International Woman

When I look at you I see magic.

All the hopes and dreams of powerful creation. The only matter that matters to me, carrying souls from the spiritual world to here, and onto their next destinations.

The world seeks to destroy you, if they can't hold you, without force, they want to control you.

All men come from you and love you so much, they'll spend the rest of their lives trying to get back inside of you.

Unbeknown that you live in them, hating you, they are hating themselves as all men are half woman.

Our scrotums were formed from labia, and our testes were ovaries. We have nipples because we all started out as women.

So men are scared of you. Especially those with pheomelanin. Many have pillaged for hundreds of years, all the while they had wives, but they wanted to dominate the creation of life itself.

No more! Your kings are waking up and we will literally die to defend you. All who will not die for you, are not kings but fallen men who you don't need or want to. Until they realize we cannot rise without you, we are useless.

In ancient times, we called god mother/father god because intelligence says the male can't conceive a man being balanced of his own.

Now these foolish men are praising father, son, and ghost. They killed you, yet they expect to live a normal life when they removed a part of themselves from their belief systems.

History was never herstory.

Men and our egos, when will we find balance?

[41] Went into a virtual reality, Nov. '17

CHROMOSOMES

I have trouble finding love due to two
qualities I possess; my
mother's paranoia and my father's
tendency to leave. So even if
love was trying to catch me, I wouldn't
be able to stay for too long.

[43] Played laser tag, Nov. '17

|NICKTIONARY|
religion: to tie back; to hold back; to thwart from forward progress; to bind.

‹random post #23›
If DNA is the software then who's the programmer?

Last Flower Moon

The *first* <u>stroke</u> was the spontaneous combustion of hydrogen playing cards with oxygen and a burst of elements seeped out of thin air.

A mixing of colors placed together on a drywall of imagination, and sealed with Buddha's blessing, were cremated into open psalms, as laughing essences left treadmarks on the shadows of minutes being used for purposeful reasons yet to be discovered.

The *second* <u>breath</u> was calming and sweet, with a hint of Cali in the back of my lungs.

Structured and composed, yet so elegant and free, opened her buds and began blossoming into one of the most beautiful of forthcomings. Basking in your ambiance helped me innerstand the meaning of true patience once again.

The *third* <u>cessation</u> learned me to a process of being a role model and big brother on end.

In her chrysalis stage, the little caterpillar's shell began to crack from outward forces that put whelps on its majestic transition in nature. Time was at a standstill, but pressure make diamonds more luminous in the end.

The *fourth* <u>exhale</u> broke free an unyielding angel ready to spread her wings on the grand stage.

With a destination in mind and good fortune in her pocket took off to face the future one yellow brick at a time. And when I glanced back at that empty shell on the ground, I almost shed a tear. Here lies the remnants of the baby caterpillar who'll grow up throughout the years

[45] Chilled with Suav, Jan. '18

REFLECTIONS

I have this fear that one day
I won't be able to make you
smile like I do now. And that
someday you'll tell me it was
great in the beginning, but I
don't love you anymore. And
that will be my tragic end.

[47] Finished book, Mar. '18

HALF PAST MIDNIGHT

I love the 3 AM version of people.
Their vulnerability. Their honesty.
The beautiful bareness underneath
their tongues keeping the algid air
vibrant.

POSTCARDS

Whenever I travel I always get tripped out
at the fact that it's someone's hometown.
Like they know every back road and how to
get everywhere and they've had tons of
memories in this city.
And I'm just someone passing by.

[50] Visited Colorado, Apr. '18

CONSTELLATIONS

I wonder, do the stars look at us the same
way we look at them? The most beautiful
as we are dying.

[52] Went on a dolphin watch, Jul. '18

[55] Went indoor skydiving, Feb. '19

Lullaby on Saint Ave.

On a brisk ride with the full moon resting
atop my shadow, my temples rattle my
chakras sending my inner poles into a
state of temporary calefaction.

It was raining, not ferociously, but a mild
temperament of trouble and joy.

It was a starry night and I waved to the
neighbors eons away as if they were right
beside me.

And I took out a notepad and began the
chorus to the softest song never spoken.

It reads; if I ever happen to write a
story about a boy, who suffers from
abandonment and loneliness, then I hope
I'm writing a lullaby.
It'll have symphonies hidden in between
the lines of somber regrets and almost is
never enough.
It'll explain how things keep going left no
matter how far right I turn, or how the
quicksand never seems to stop falling.
It'll tell of mischief, disbelief, serendipity,
retrogression, and pain.
It'll break down the playground prisons
caging my inner self into the state of
hopelessness.
It'll carry my burdens on its shoulders and
parade them around for the world to see.

It'll help me cry, because deep within I
feel as if I should.
It'll heal me, and promise a better tomorrow
is to come, just as long as I embraced the
sunset on the horizon.
It'll speak the words I have trouble forming,
with expressions I feel are too vulgar to
withstand alone.
It'll help me wonder as to why I feel the
emotions of others, yet still have to
question my own persuasions.
It'll show the correct lens in the kaleidoscopic
photo frame.

And, when I get to the last sentence, it'll
catch all the tears I shuffled away to write
this orchestra.
The octaves of humiliation,
the weeping-bells of forgotten ills,
the final recording in the sand.
At peace, I see a new day!

ULTRAVIOLET

Since that night, I found myself drawn
to your light like a moth, with the over
whelming desire to enter the flames
just to feel something.

My skin is crawling again and there
are earthquakes in my chest with no
where to go. How can you provoke in
me a hurricane of feelings just by
looking into my eyes?

I can't phrase emotions into phrases
that you may comprehend. To be at
your side is a privilege that I do not
deserve, but still would like to have.

|NICKTIONARY|
kakistocracy: a form of government in which the
worst people are in power

EMPTY PROMISES

Unrequited love is a bittersweet tragedy. How the
heart just wants something it can never have.
Like,
how a tree bows down to the roaring winds; the
tree breaks down before it and gives everything
to the wind.
How it'll say "take everything for I will
love you always." Yet, the wind whispers back after
the storm and says sorrowfully,
"I'm sorry, I can never love you in this way.
But I am forever grateful for this."
And still, the crestfallen tree stays rooted.

THE DEEP END

What a culture we live in.
People are swimming in an
ocean of information, yet
found the time to drown
in a puddle of ignorance.

QTNA

All my life I never
understood why you
left so soon... why you
never even tried.
It wasn't even storming,
just overcast with a
chance of rain.

. . .

Let me go down on your mind while I softly suck
on your thoughts; sliding my tongue into the
wetness of your intellect, and circling the clit
of your emotions. I want to savor all of your
intimate disclosures, doing it slow and deep;
soul kissing the entrance of your secrets. I just
want to gently suck on the nib of your determination,
and make your mindgasm on the tongue of my
intelligence.

RUFFLED PAGES

I am an open book who's
pages tell stories never
thought imaginable. I
however, can't be read
until someone shows
interest in my story.
I am a mixed tape of
aeonian melodies, but
no one owns a cassette
player anymore. So I
sing heart songs at
the cusp of dawn,
waiting for the day my
energy reservoirs break
free and deplete the
status quo.

[56] Signed book contract, Apr. '19

I Wanna Fuck to the Red Light

Aboriginal war cries are beginning to heat
up the cemented cracks subdued in the
concrete jungles of overpopulated cesspools

The statutes of a government which no longer
sheds in skin in secrecy leaves indoctrinated
misconceptions smeared all over the landmass

Anhedonic lifestyles reproduce hypersexual
offspring who can no longer bear the opposite
sex, causing communication to fail with every
lol text sent

A red flag is drawn on the gameplay once
thought so complex, now being rewoven
through the cat strings of determined nations

A man who once stood at the gates of
imperial design, or so he says, tucks his tail
and cowers behind his long range barrel
cloaked in chaos as nature begins to rewrite
the declaration of natural rights

Goosebumped bronze skins transform into
reflective armors ready to burst at the
slightest movement of rash crawling viruses

Because as a targeted population is
continually criminalized and dehumanized
in society, their lives become trophies as
if they belong plastered or outlined in
chalk

Body after body are stuffed and dismantled,
traveling miles underground from home
until their carcasses rot into past memories

Crooked con artist are hinted as key suspects
simply because the inconsistency falling from
their tongues can't keep pace with their nocent
actions carried out on innocent civilians

And we have the audacity to put out hands up
Fuck that! Throw those arms around one another
and clench those fist into history making wrecking balls

Break the cycle we need a government to
guide us into salvation The corporation made
it clear numbers don't hold weight, and
are easily erasable as digitized calculations

Cease the chemical warfare plaguing colorful
communities as if they were Z-class citizens

Because the grass may be greener on the
other side but the sewer lined water kills the
growing gold underneath

Cease the obstruction of younger minds being
molded into nihilistic, cannibalistic, fascist socio
robots programmed to forget that childhoods
only come around once a lifetime

Kill the stockholm syndrome symptoms that allow
the passive aggressive gentrifiers to constantly
push away children of the sun closer to their
demise

Ready round up the cattle since it's chow time
then stick tags on the ears and lock them
in gates. Order the pigs to protect the bank so
the farmer can cash out on stocks of another
quiet hero

Where are the inventive minds and speakers
that architect the future of innovation?

Why must there only be mistrust and envy when
I drop my vernacular so fluently on minds
succumbed to the evils of mass manipulation?

I'll bet my answer on the stars, who sit so
distant but remain so far, falling down on
the whim of a prayer, to bring illumination
on a decaying age

TIMEKEEPER

Some humans are born with birds
inside their bodies and that's
why some bones resemble cages.
But concealed beneath my ribs
lay a dragon, trying to see how
much smoke my body can take
before oxygen becomes impossible
to swallow.

[57] Climbed first lighthouse, May '19

ONYX

I won't apologize for being a warrior
because you made me this way. I have
turned my skin into armor that deflects
crude judgments and inevitable rejection.
I must fight for myself because who else
will?

I can't be saved,
I've already saved myself.

So don't become flustered when I put up my
shield. I've yet to understand a tender touch.
I am neither beautiful, nor soft. I am power!
Because,
I have no other choice but to be!

LUNCH BREAK

My hands wet yet my arms clean,
I'm not supposed to be knee deep in shit,
She said you must yet I couldn't see,
I'm not trying to get in over my head here,
half the time she's begging please.

My response was a firm no,
her yes was so calm,
it almost made me rethink.

As far as I'm concerned,
I did what I had to so we can say it can't be.
Maybe never again after,
the fact is I'm keeping my heart clean.
If they found out it'll be a disaster,
in one way or another, I have to put my
mistress to sleep.

WINDOWPANE

Not every morning is a blessing for me.
They're days I arise with no hope,
peace, or love.
Just a sense of dread that I am still alive
in this godforsaken world

<random post #13>

Nostalgia, whether it be bad or good, always leaves
a tiny bit of emptiness afterwards

INN(h)ER GLOW

All she ever saw was
darkness within herself.
I wish I could make her
see the light, with which
she brightened other
people's lives.

What's in a Name?

FLASHPOINT

I look around and see colors and
people, fading in and out, like a
camera lens that struggles to focus.
Then the shutter dims, and they're
left in a blindness of their own
makings.

GALACTIC DESCENDANT

We are born of the stars.
From the cataclysmic beginning of the universe
came the first cells, comprised of stardust and
dark matter and happenstance. And by means
of adaptation, and natural selection, humans
were formed.

A mere collection of cells we are, stumbling
through life as one would stumble through a
cave as black as pitch; blindly, with open
hands outstretched in the darkness, clinging to
some feeble hope of finding direction.

Deep in the marrow of our bones, we long to
rejoin the macrocosm. We long to return to our
primordial state.

And when we die, we are once again born of
the stars.

INSUFFICIENT FUNDS

I was too much for her and she wasn't enough for
me. We grew apart before we could even fall for
each other

She always said I was not like other guys
That it was the first time for her to meet a
soul like mine in this world

She wasn't able to read me, or guess what I was
thinking
when I looked at her.

I was a puzzle she couldn't decipher
and in the end, she got tired of playing riddles

She wanted a love where she could understand my
heart
but I wasn't able to give it to her.
I was too much and she wasn't enough for me.

I did love her, but another part of me always
looked the other way
Looking for something deeper than what she can offer
me.

I couldn't recognize her soul even if I wanted to
Despite that, we tried to be happy together while
denying the obvious

I know, we were never meant to be
but I still love her, and I will for awhile.

Nich

<u>NOCTURNAL</u>

I'm a paradox.
Meaning I am he who wants to be happy,
but will ponder things that'll make me
worrisome.

I'm lazy, yet ambiguous,
so at times I don't appreciate myself,
but deep down, I also love who I am.

I say I don't care, knowing DAMN well I do.

I sometimes crave attention, but will detach
myself from those who're right in front of my
face.

I'm a conflicted contradiction,
who hasn't figured himself out yet.
And because of that, I hope no one else has
too.

Age of Pisces

There's a war in the immune system for the
knowledge of self,
and in that environment,
is what we depend on for our understanding
of life.

We live amongst soulless avatars, who's only
purpose is to attenuate
indigo vessels out of their
ether waveforms, so that their energy reservoirs
may break the shield placed atop the
firmament.

The webbed lies above trapped us in this
twilight zone of shape
shifting mirages, thought
plausible threw everyday causes and natural
phenomena.

And here we speak of world war 3, as if
those seconds are miles
away from the shortcomings of tomorrow's
cri de coeur.

So we pray to a g.o.d. who glorifies the misery,
masked in nihilistic
propaganda, until the death toll
comes knocking at your front door, and
you wonder if this is the bases
of martial law.

But who's really paying attention to the
cards on the table?
We're being mined for a mind
who sees us as errs to the plantation,
with greedy overseers, and
their vaunting behaviors.

With a controlled ideology invested in
artificial moira, given to
us as we forfeit to the temptations,
burning our feet to a crisp on the tar conveyor
belt, that pulls us all to our demise
slowly.

While coastal dominions are burning outside
in, due to the
interference of governing
officials and their weapons of biological
insemination.

Code red police states are bringing in the
troops, to replace human
populace with intelligent cyborgs
capable of reprogramming the matrix.

An infiltration of the physical realm roams
pass indoctrinated eyes
subdued in the desensitized world
we know of today.

From an unknown push by a covert enemy
who harnessed the
energy of the mother, as we
pushed to make our "ends meet."

And the questions we wondered are becoming
cloudy, as the metals
above our heads come crashing
down like the lies we were fed as young
light transcendents.

So don't believe everything you see,
because their camouflage
technique is damn near flawless,
and the eyes of the beast hides many
secrets.

Be wary of the halo projection…

JAGGED EDGE

When it was time for battle,
I sheath my sword to use
my words as the weapons,
and my isolation was the shield
So that I can damage others
when things get intense, but no
one can damage me when all
seem to fall down

LIGHTERS UP

This goes out to the ones who are left grieving
And for those of whom are in their loneliest of
phases
This is for my broken hearted homeland
And people who are affected by natural disasters
This goes to the new immigrants by the thousands
And the refugees who follow not too far behind

This is for the ill-gotten blues, with broken hearts,

And people who tend to keep trying their hardest,
Yet seem to fail every time
Its for those forgotten people
And people who want to forget as much as they can
Those of whom 2018 will be their starting page

And for those of whom 2018 will be the last breath

M.A.R.S

Approximately ten years ago is when I would start to lose my
light, from a devastating impact that completely altered my life.
My friend went insane due to complications of the brain, which
in deed buried my heart in
my father's land
I'll fast forward, let's say a smooth seventy-two, to when things
became a bit more iniquitous. You see, things kinda went left

because, my sister's last breath was spent spewing out hatred and utter chagrin.

We ended up in a cell and for her it was hell, but nothing prepared us for what was to come later. I would lose my best friend, I would lose my motivation, and I used up all that was left in a tiny prayer.

I took a short ride that felt like forever to an island disconnected from the cultures surrounding it. I was met by a guard who signed me to stay and closed the door to my new placement. That night I tried to cry, but crying wasn't on the itinerary.

So instead, I held myself, until my mind felt at ease once again. Only this time I wouldn't realize the scars I grew would eventually cage me in. I was placed in a jail that was built with no bars, yet we needed permission to go out and freelance. I fought with my words, although I wrapped up my fist, and understood the hierarchy at hand.

Either eat or be eaten, defend or be beaten, that crying is for weaklings, and niggas stay schemin'.

A ten month tenure would soon change at a dinner, where I would be sold to a parent of the highest bidder. My transition went quick, I was placed in the sticks, with a commando, two nerds, and a man who rarely cooked dinner. One would become like my brother, whom I'll love like no other, and help guide me through my troubled youth. It was from his teachings, and real world reasoning, that showed me the hidden truths.

Two years of my life, consisted of turmoil and strife, as I pledged to finally return home. Unknown to my senses, that being stuck in the system, took a toll on me, but also my siblings.

My might had been tested, my spirit was restless, and my freedumb papers had finally come. I was 16-years-old, with a heart full of cold, ready to embrace the new coming sun. So I went home for a while, yes only a while, because things went wrong judicially.

Nich

I go back for a week, or so I was I was told, why, for reasons left completely unattended. I agree to the terms, and waited my time, only to be stuck reminiscing. That week turned into eight which then multiplied by four, and a
year was hanging in the balance.
Things wouldn't go right, in my fucked up life, and soon my nocent behaviors protested. I was caught up in the game, not realising my hand, and eventually I got
myself arrested.
I was given an option to not be forgotten, but ultimately I couldn't leave the state. At least not for a year, and not even with peers, unless I wished to see that metal gate. I was losing my touch and didn't give a fuck, because a fuck didn't cry for me. I had to carry myself and watch my own back because my existence was taking
up space.
She put me outside and fed me to the wolves and said I had to make my own plate. I wanted to cry, I swear deep inside, but tears don't come empty handed. I was seventeen at this point, emotions were stirring, and I swear I just wanted some answers. My luck had ran out, my
mom she gave up, and once again I was
completely abandoned.
I was placed on the street, with no one to bother me, finished high school, and went to New Orleans.
That berceuse summer was by far one of the best. I began feeling happy, I would learn about my nest. I was becoming a man and no tears could seem to stop me at least not until I saw my family leave that college lobby.
I attended a school, supposedly to help strengthen my roots, found me some friends, and called em "DA CREW." That winter is what inspired me to write more, I was down four, tapped out and ran poor.
But I stayed strong, packed bags and went home, talked turkey and realised it's the same song.
It was lame too, my legs hurt, my brain bruised.

I got that displacement letter, and with
no cheddar, I shred school.
I had to call it quits before diving off the deep end, return to sender, and then bury my new friends. I needed a nap but, my dreams kept me from sleeping and there I was in that city, for no apparent reason
My anger grew, my hair locked, and I changed my mood, I took some time to myself, wanting nothing to do with school. I got a job, became depressed and looked above, saw a beacon for testing and reached for it without
thought.
It was then I caught on to why I skipped school, why I moved packs and why I stayed rude. I just needed an escape, before all was too late, because I lacked a loving support which made me irate.
I put out my last blunt and went on a search to find out who I am destined to meet. It just so happen I discovered some rings and innerstood I was looking for me. So I meditated and waited until my vision became clear, and when I opened my eye, the world was without fear.
I went on a cleanse to help wash away my sins, broke bread with my enemies, and touched palms with old friends. To the road less traveled, where I fell twice in battle, but things will be different next time.
I reached for the stars and traveled afar, throwing my failures away. I wrote off my problems and locked them up tightly and sat out towards the bay.
On the eve of my heartbreak, dated two years later, I returned to my home by the sea. With my consciousness growing and spirit overflowing I embodied an entire
new scene.
I spoke with a purpose and laughed with a cause, I threw house parties, and traversed the tars. I helped those who needed, and learned those who didn't, while a crystal heart with amethyst grew attached to my pendant I learned my twin flame and watched the widow peak. I went back and forth to court to set

What's in a Name?

my testimony free. Ended up writing a few psalms, got in touch
with beyond, saw through my third eye, then suppressed the
raging storms.
At twenty-two, things were smooth, and life pointed me in the
direction of a clue. Which was to buy black the block, and invest
in stock, in order to multiply revenue. Proclaim my true name so
that I won't end up detained, and eventually go back to school.
And here I stand, alive, reassuring my position as I progress
further along my path. The mirror is still foggy as I gaze into it,
and I often drift off staring at the world
through my rearview.
And if my synopsis is correct then, maybe, I'm scared of the
inevitable, wrapped in a layer of surprises, bound to a
constitution that writs my protection valid
and transcendental.

[59] GoKarts, archery, mini golf & pottery, Baeday '19

|NICKTIONARY|

calcination: the time in our lives when we start seeing the
tricks, illusions, misleading beliefs, and harmful habits of
our egos and put them aside so we can finally explore
what lies underneath.

[60] Started book club, Jun. '19

Sombali Visions

Celebrations are in order
as the hands of the father
begin to wind down from
the ills of the precipice
world.
New horizons busticate
beyond the sunrays
unveiling an aberration
of yesterday's common
misconceptions, pushing
hyetal afternoons into
a corner of Pandora's
box.
These quivering emotions
banding together help
to decide if today is truly
constitutional.
Will a name be etched
into
the clamor of the wind?
Or will the circumferential,
benighted population
wage war of the ideology
of enlightenment?
Perhaps, it's time to invest
in this inceptive obstacle
course and take note
of
the lessons unearthed.

So here is where I lay
down my sword, exhaling
the eurythmic
expressions that begin
the soundtrack to my
paseo journey.

|NICKTIONARY|

dystopia: a society characterized by human misery,
as squalor, oppression, disease, and overcrowding.

[62] Went to D.C., Aug. '19

XANADU

A gift of the physical,
awakening sixth senses,
a state of being in which,
there are no coincidences.

Preceded not by solid touch,
but trust so divine,
a joining of souls,
a meeting of the minds

[67] IT'S A GIRL !!

My Twenty Two degrees of reparations

What's in a Name?

Nich

Author's Bio

Nich,

short for Nicholis, is bred from New Orleans, Louisiana. From early childhood obstacles such as the displacement with hurricane Katrina, a family feud that nearly separated loved ones permanently, abandonment by a parent, and coming of age in the foster care system of New York City, made him the man he is today. With a minor in classroom academics, the world became his teacher, as he learns to understand exactly what's in a name.

Nich

colophon
Brought to you by Wider Perspectives Publishing, care of James
Wilson, with the mission of advancing the poetry and creative
community of Hampton Roads, Virginia.
See our production of works from …

Tanya Cunningham
        (Scientific Eve)
Terra Leigh
Ray Simmons Samantha
Borders-Shoemaker
Taz Waysweete'
Bobby K.
        (The Poor Man's Poet)
J. Scott Wilson (TEECH!)
Charles Wilson
Gloria Darlene Mann
Neil Spirtas

Zach Crowe
Jorge Mendez & JT Williams
Sarah Eileen Williams
        Stephanie Diana (Noftz)
the Hampton Roads
        Artistic Collective
Jason Brown (Drk Mtr)
Martina Champion
Tony Broadway
Ken Sutton
Crickyt J. Expression
Lisa Kendrick
Cassandra IsFree

… and others to come soon.

We promote and support the artists of the 757
  from the seats, from the stands,
  from the snapping fingers and clapping hands
  from the pages, and the stages
  and now we pass them forth to the ages

Check for the above artists on FaceBook, the Virginia Poetry Online
channel on YouTube, and other social media.

Hampton Roads Artistic Collective is the non-profit extension of WPP
and strives to simultaneously support worthy causes in Hampton Roads
and the creative artists.

www.ingramcontent.com/pod-product-compliance
Lightning Source LLC
Chambersburg PA
CBHW040513290326
41930CB00036B/113